SRA Early Interventions in Reading

Level 1

Answer Key

MHEonline.com

SRA

Columbus, OH 43240-4027

Printed in the United States of America.

Columbus, OH

The **McGraw·Hill** Companies

MHEonline.com

 SRA

Imprint 2012
Copyright © 2005 by SRA/McGraw-Hill.

Send all inquiries to:
SRA/McGraw-Hill
8787 Orion Place
Columbus, OH 43240-4027

Printed in the United States of America.

ISBN 0-07-602668-X

15 16 17 LHN 21 20 19

The McGraw·Hill Companies

Table of Contents

Table of Contents

Lesson 1

m

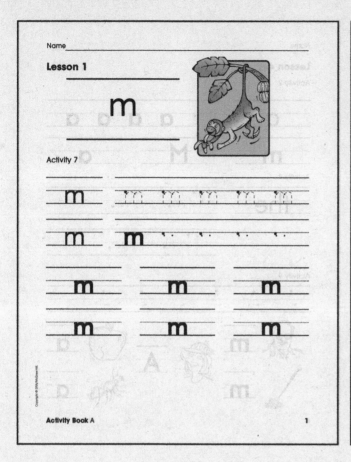

Activity 7

m   m m m

m   m

m   m   m

m   m   m

Lesson 2

Activity 5

If I Were a Mouse

If I were a mouse,
a mouse, a mouse,
I'd never live in
a house, a house;
I'd live outside
where grass grows tall,
With other mouse
friends big and small.

Lesson 2

Activity 6

M   M M M M M

M   M

Activity 9

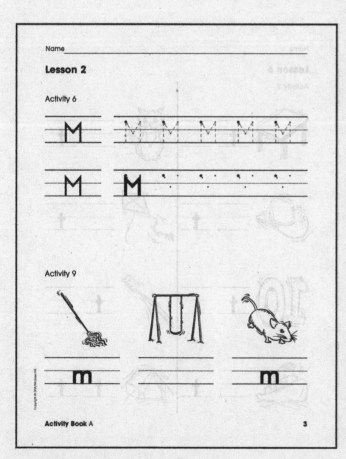

m   m

Lesson 2

Activity 10

m   m

m   m

m   m

m   m

Name _____

Lesson 3

a

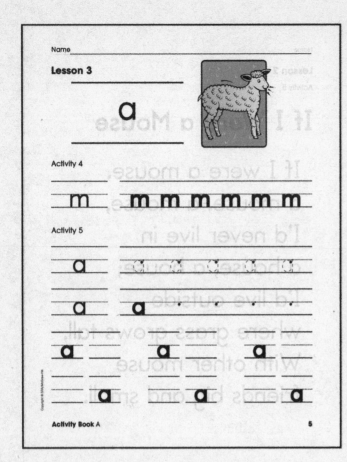

Activity 4

m   m m m m m m

Activity 5

a   a

a   a

a   a

a   a   a   a

Name _____

Lesson 4

Activity 2

a   a a a a

m   M   a

Activity 4

the   the   the

the   the

Activity 9

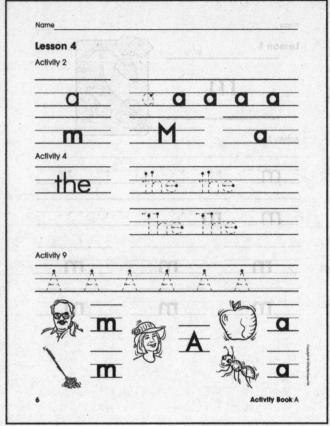

m

m   A   a

Name _____

Lesson 5

t

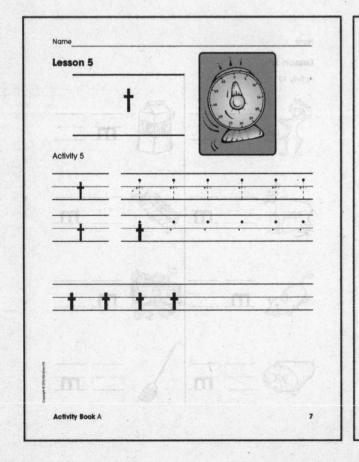

Activity 5

t   t   t   t   t   t

t   t

t   t   t   t

Name _____

Lesson 6

Activity 2

t   t

t   t

t   t

t   t

Lesson 6

Activity 3

Activity 6

am   at

Activity 7

I am

Lesson 7

s

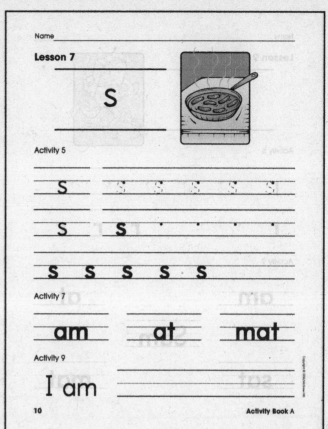

Activity 5

s   s   s   s   s   s

s   s   .   .   .   .

s   s   s   s   s

Activity 7

am   at   mat

Activity 9

I am

Lesson 8

Activity 2

s   s   s   s   s   s

s

s

s

s

Lesson 8

Activity 5

is   is   b   is

Activity 6

a   m

s   t

Activity 7

am   at

ma   sa

Answer Key Activity Book A

Lesson 9

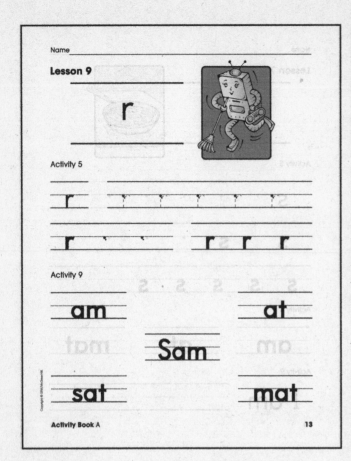

r

Activity 5

r

r   r r r

Activity 9

am   at

Sam

sat   mat

Lesson 10

Activity 3

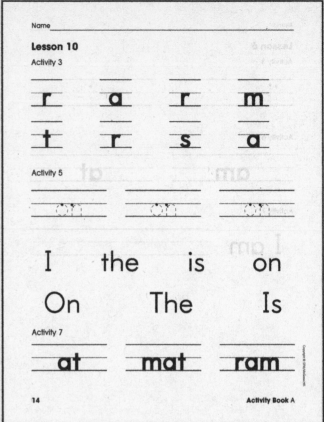

r   a   r   m

t   r   s   a

Activity 5

on   on   on

I   the   is   on

On   The   Is

Activity 7

at   mat   ram

Lesson 11

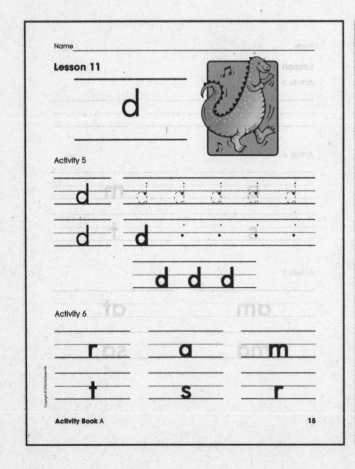

d

Activity 5

d

d   d

d d d

Activity 6

r   a   m

t   s   r

Lesson 12

Activity 5

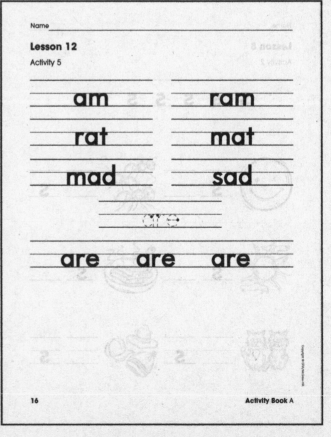

am   ram

rat   mat

mad   sad

are   are   are

Name_____

Lesson 13
_____

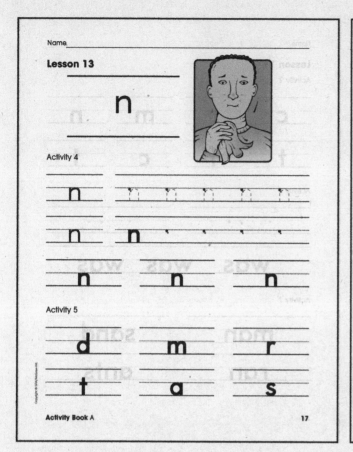

n

Activity 4

n   n n n n n

n   n

n   n   n

Activity 5

d   m   r

t   a   s

Activity Book A   17

Name_____

Lesson 14
Activity 4

mat   rat

Nat

sad   mad

Activity 6

have   have

Activity 8

I am Sam.

I am a rat.

I have a ram.

18   **Activity Book A**

Name_____

Lesson 15
_____

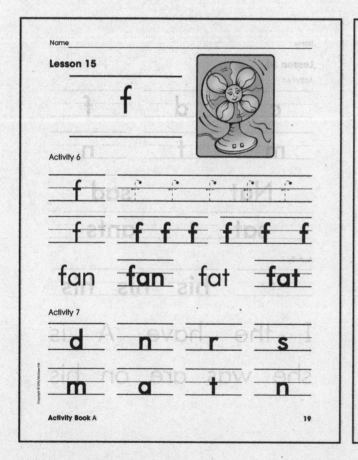

f

Activity 6

f   f f f f f

f   f f f f f

fan   fan   fat   fat

Activity 7

d   n   r   s

m   a   t   n

Activity Book A   19

Name_____

Lesson 16
Activity 4

f   n   d   f

m   n   f   t

Activity 6

fan   Nan   man

ran   fat   Nat

Activity 7

she

she   she   she

20   **Activity Book A**

Answer Key Activity Book A   **5**

Name

Lesson 17

Activity 3

c					
c	c				
f		s		n	d
a		m		r	t

Activity 8

fan	fast
ram	sand

Name

Lesson 18

Activity 2

c	r	m	n
t	f	c	t

Activity 4

was	was

was   was   was

Activity 7

man	sand
ran	ants

Name

Lesson 19

i

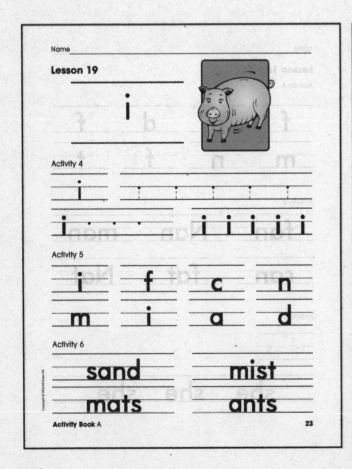

Activity 4

i					
i			i	i	i i

Activity 5

i		f	c	n
m		i	a	d

Activity 6

sand	mist
mats	ants

Name

Lesson 20

Activity 6

c	d	f
m	t	n

Nat	sad
sat	ants

Activity 7

his   his   his   his

I   the   have   A   is

she   was   are   on   his

Lesson 21
Activity 4

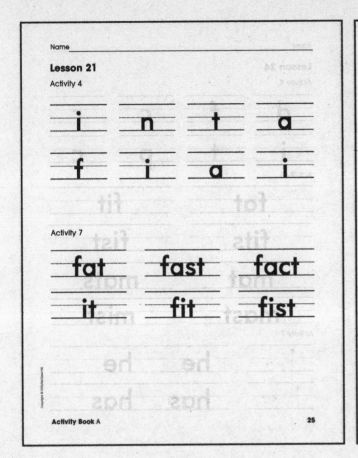

i   n   t   a
f   i   a   i

Activity 7

fat   fast   fact
it   fit   fist

Lesson 22
Activity 4

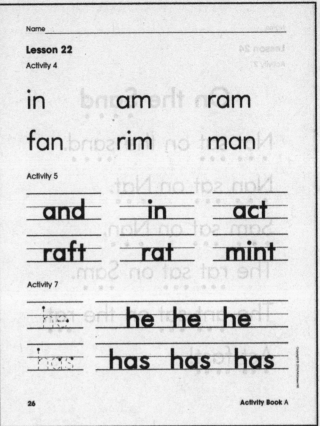

in   am   ram
fan   rim   man

Activity 5

and   in   act
raft   rat   mint

Activity 7

he   he   he
has   has   has

Lesson 23

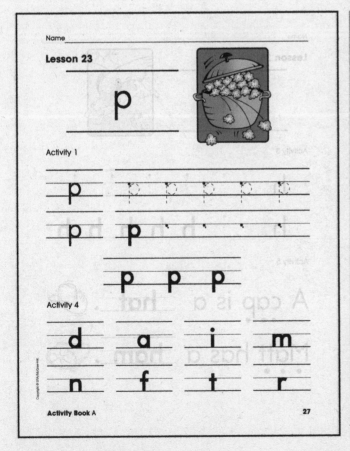

p

Activity 1

p   p p p p p
p   p

p p p

Activity 4

d   a   i   m
n   f   t   r

Lesson 23
Activity 6

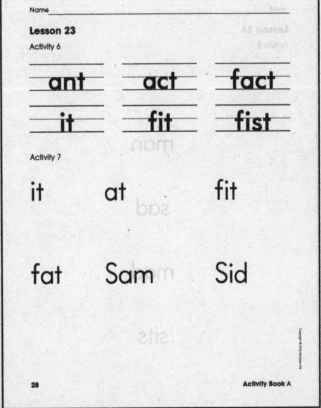

ant   act   fact
it   fit   fist

Activity 7

it   at   fit

fat   Sam   Sid

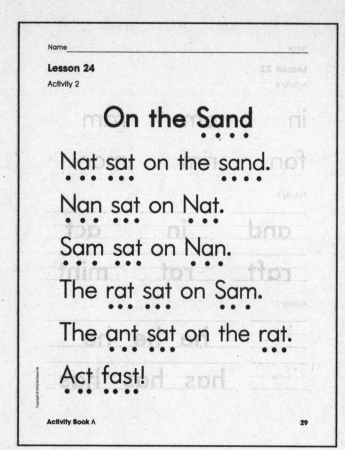

Name

Lesson 24

Activity 2

On the Sand

Nat sat on the sand.

Nan sat on Nat.

Sam sat on Nan.

The rat sat on Sam.

The ant sat on the rat.

Act fast!

Activity Book A   29

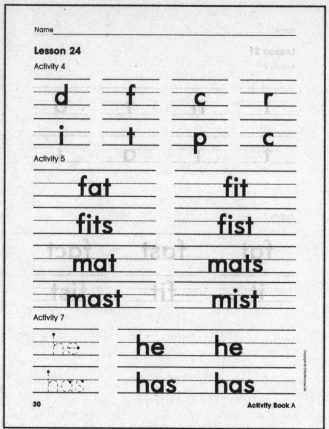

Name

Lesson 24

Activity 4

d	f	c	r
i	t	p	c

Activity 5

fat	fit
fits	fist
mat	mats
mast	mist

Activity 7

he	he	he
has	has	has

30   **Activity Book** A

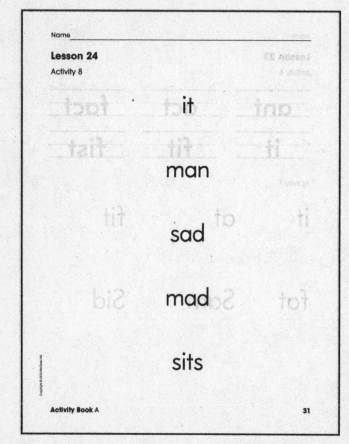

Name

Lesson 24

Activity 8

it

man

sad

mad

sits

Activity Book A   31

Name

Lesson 25

h

Activity 3

h

h   h h h h h

Activity 5

A cap is a   hat .

Matt has a   ham .

32   **Activity Book** A

8

Answer Key Activity Book A

Lesson 26
Activity 3

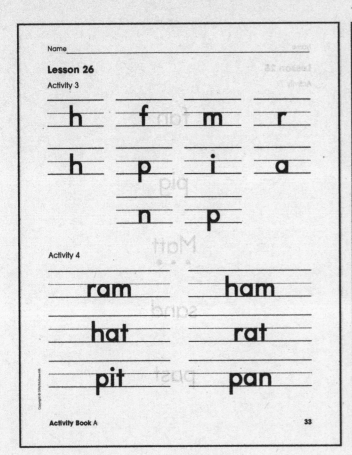

h f m r

h p i a

n p

Activity 4

ram   ham

hat   rat

pit   pan

Lesson 26
Activity 6

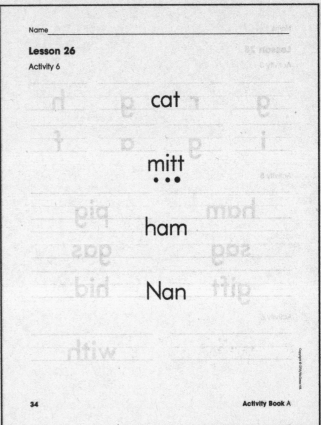

cat

mitt
• • •

ham

Nan

Lesson 27
Activity 1

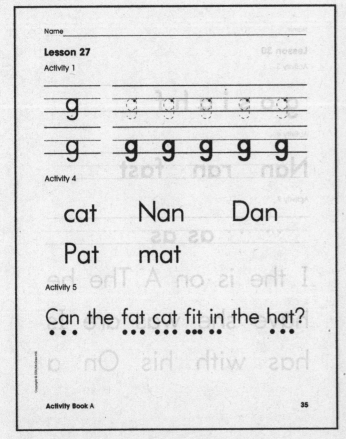

g

g   g g g g g

Activity 4

cat   Nan   Dan

Pat   mat

Activity 5

Can the fat cat fit in the hat?
• • •   • • • • • • • • • •   • • •

Lesson 27
Activity 6

Sid **did** a handstand.   did / dad

Nan sat on the **hat**.   hit / hat

Sam has a **pan**.   pin / pan

Answer Key Activity Book A

9

Lesson 28
Activity 3

| g | r | g | h |
| i | g | a | f |

Activity 5

ham	pig
sag	gas
gift	hid

Activity 6

with   **with**

Activity Book A   **37**

Lesson 28
Activity 7

fan

pig

Matt
• • •

sand

past

38   **Activity Book** A

Lesson 29

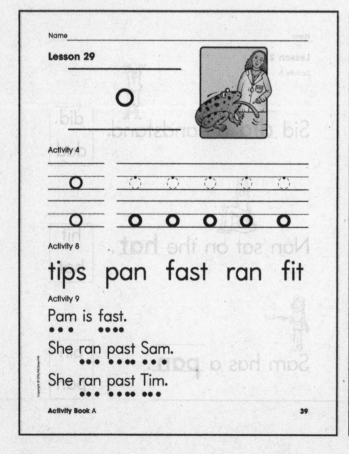

O

Activity 4

O ⦾ ⦾ ⦾ ⦾ ⦾

O O O O O O

Activity 8

tips pan fast ran fit

Activity 9

Pam is fast.
• • • • • • •

She ran past Sam.
• • • • • • • • • •

She ran past Tim.
• • • • • • • • • •

Activity Book A   **39**

Lesson 30
Activity 3

g o s i a h f

Activity 4

Nan ran fast

Activity 7

as as **as as**

I the is on A The he
have she was are Is
has with his On a

40   **Activity Book** A

Name

Lesson 31

sh

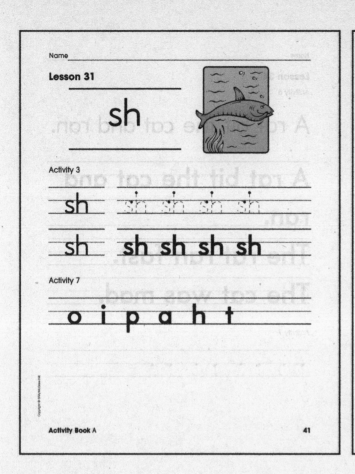

Activity 3

sh | sh sh sh sh
sh | **sh sh sh sh**

Activity 7

o i p a h t

Name

Lesson 31

Activity 8

hat   Pam
camp   hats
rot

Activity 10

The cat had a nap on a mat.

The rat hit the cat and ran.

The rat ran fast.

Name

Lesson 32

Activity 4

shop   ship
pin   camp
fish

Activity 6

had   mitt

cat   fish

Name

Lesson 33

b

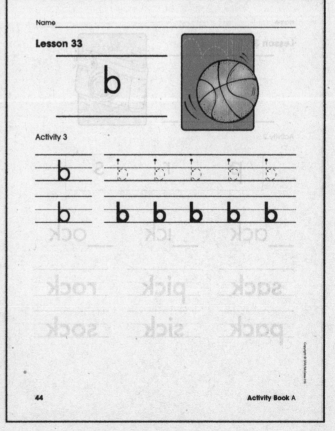

Activity 3

b | b b b b b
b | **b b b b b**

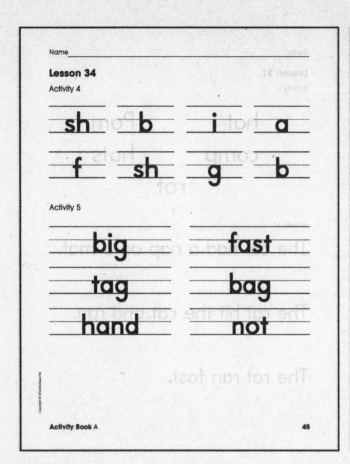

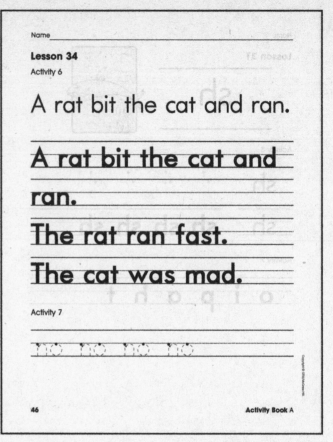

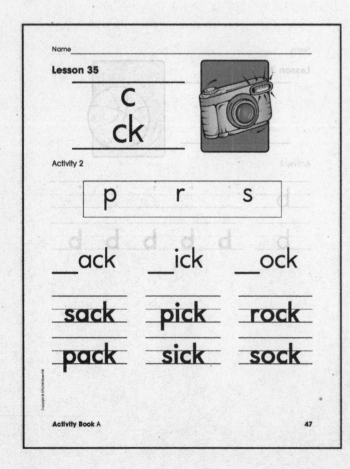

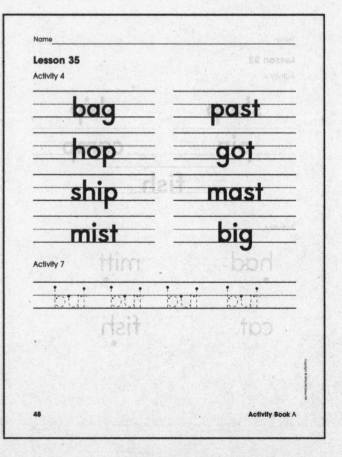

Panel 1 (top left):

Name

Lesson 34

Activity 4

| sh | b | i | a |
| f | sh | g | b |

Activity 5

big	fast
tag	bag
hand	not

Panel 2 (top right):

Name

Lesson 34

Activity 6

A rat bit the cat and ran.

A rat bit the cat and ran.
The rat ran fast.
The cat was mad.

Activity 7

Panel 3 (bottom left):

Name

Lesson 35

c
ck

Activity 2

| p | r | s |

_ack   _ick   _ock

| sack | pick | rock |
| pack | sick | sock |

Panel 4 (bottom right):

Name

Lesson 35

Activity 4

bag	past
hop	got
ship	mast
mist	big

Activity 7

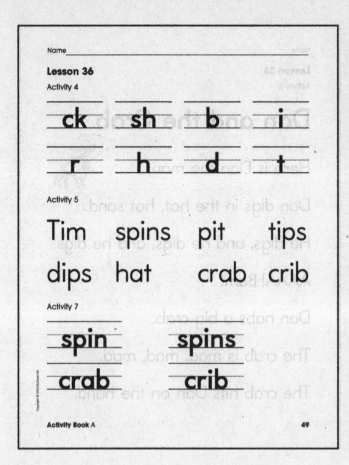

Lesson 36
Activity 4

ck	sh	b	i
r	h	d	t

Activity 5

Tim spins pit tips
dips hat crab crib

Activity 7

spin	spins
crab	crib

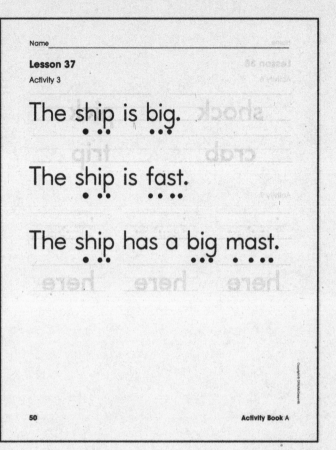

Lesson 37
Activity 3

The ship is big.
• •   • •

The ship is fast.
• •   • • •

The ship has a big mast.
• •   • • • • •

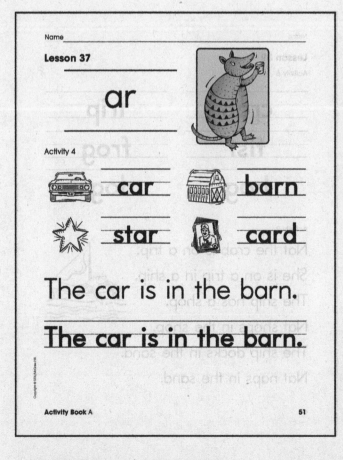

Lesson 37

ar

Activity 4

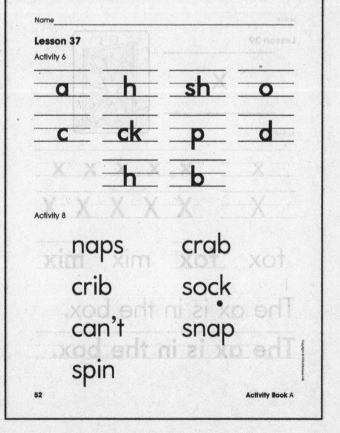 car   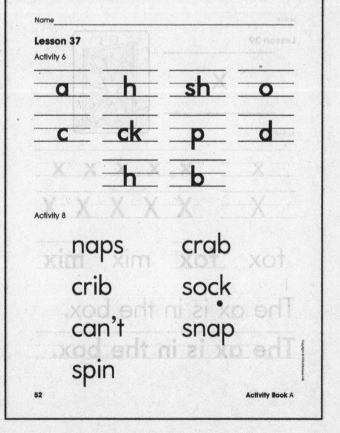 barn

  star   card

The car is in the barn.

The car is in the barn.

Lesson 37
Activity 6

a	h	sh	o
c	ck	p	d
	h	b	

Activity 8

naps   crab
crib   sock
can't   snap
spin

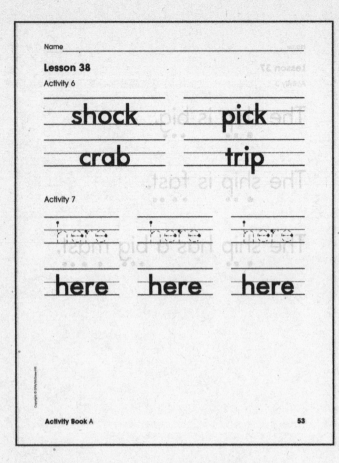

Lesson 38

Activity 6

shock   pick

crab   trip

Activity 7

here   here   here

Lesson 38

Activity 8

Dan and the Crab

Here is Dan the man.

Dan digs in the hot, hot sand.

He digs, and he digs, and he digs.

AAAA! Bam!

Dan nabs a big crab.

The crab is mad, mad, mad.

The crab hits Dan on the hand.

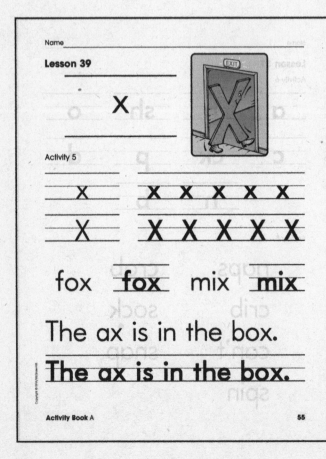

Lesson 39

X

Activity 5

X   X X X X X

X   X X X X X

fox **fox** mix **mix**

The ax is in the box.

The ax is in the box.

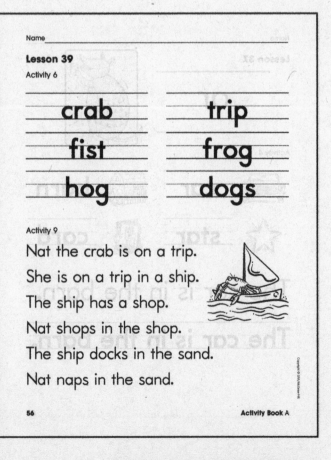

Lesson 39

Activity 6

crab   trip

fist   frog

hog   dogs

Activity 9

Nat the crab is on a trip.

She is on a trip in a ship.

The ship has a shop.

Nat shops in the shop.

The ship docks in the sand.

Nat naps in the sand.

sh   ck   c   ar

x   d   b   i

___i___   ___a___   ___o___

six   bag   mop

fist   cap   fox

pig   bat   box

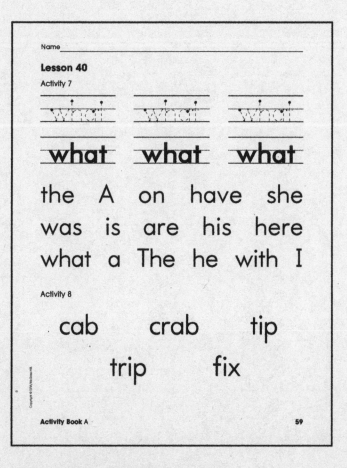

what   what   what

the   A   on   have   she

was   is   are   his   here

what   a   The   he   with   I

Activity 8

cab   crab   tip

trip   fix

Answer Key Activity Book A   **15**

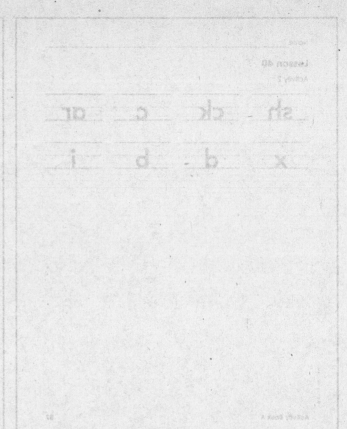

sh   ck   a   ar

x   d   b   i

o   a   i

mop   bag   six

fox   cap   fist

box   bat   pig

what   what   what

the A on have she

was is are his here

what a The he with I

Activity 8

cab   crab   tip

trip   fix

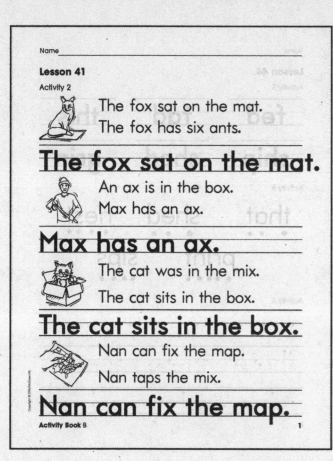

Lesson 41

Activity 2

The fox sat on the mat.
The fox has six ants.

The fox sat on the mat.

An ax is in the box.
Max has an ax.

Max has an ax.

The cat was in the mix.
The cat sits in the box.

The cat sits in the box.

Nan can fix the map.
Nan taps the mix.

Nan can fix the map.

Activity Book B   1

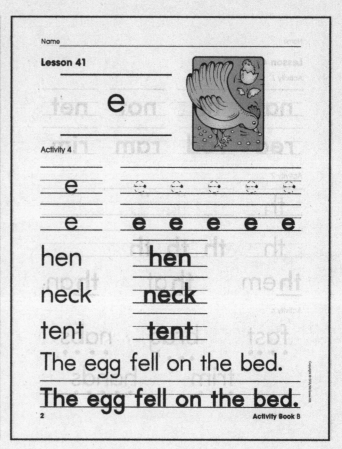

Lesson 41

e

Activity 4

e

e   e   e   e   e   e

hen   **hen**

neck   **neck**

tent   **tent**

The egg fell on the bed.

The egg fell on the bed.

2   **Activity Book B**

Lesson 41

Activity 5

x   sh   p   d

r   c   ck   ar

b   t

Activity 8

far   fox   Max

trim   ax   hot

Activity Book B   3

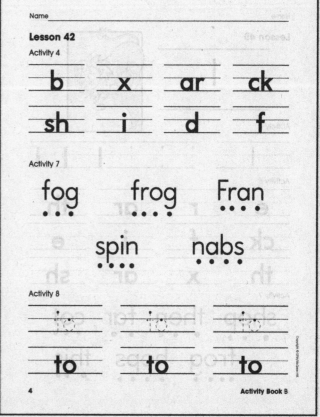

Lesson 42

Activity 4

b   x   ar   ck

sh   i   d   f

Activity 7

fog   frog   Fran

spin   nabs

Activity 8

to   to   to

4   **Activity Book B**

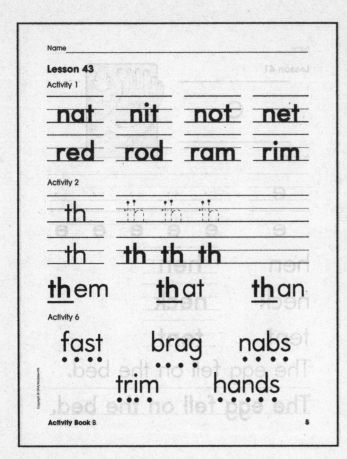

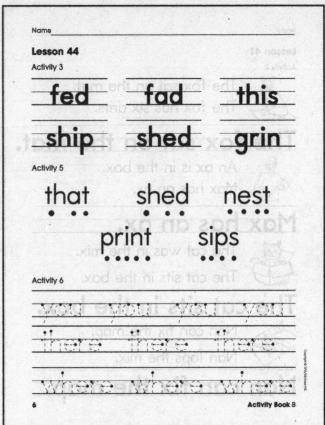

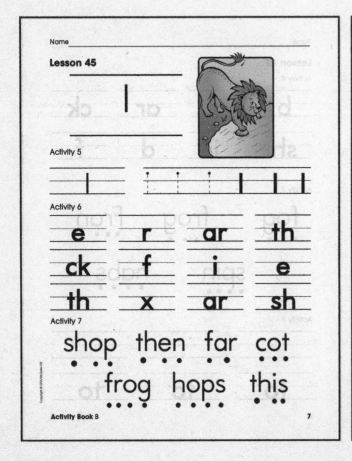

Lesson 43

Activity 1

nat nit not net

red rod ram rim

Activity 2

th

th th th th

th th th th

them **th**at **th**an

Activity 6

fast brag nabs

trim hands

Lesson 44

Activity 3

fed fad this

ship shed grin

Activity 5

that shed nest

print sips

Activity 6

Lesson 45

Activity 5

|

Activity 6

e r ar th

ck f i e

th x ar sh

Activity 7

shop then far cot

frog hops this

ar ck

Lesson 46

Activity 4

th g l r

h p d sh

b l th e

Activity 5

lock list fox

clock trap rabbit

Activity 6

yes yes **yes** **yes**

said said **said** **said**

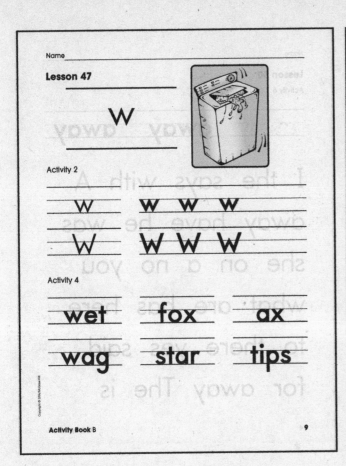

Name _____

Lesson 47
_____

W

Activity 2

W   W W W
W   W W W

Activity 4

wet   fox   ax
wag   star   tips

Activity Book B   9

Name _____

Lesson 48
Activity 2

win   wet   met
tops   taps   tips

Activity 6

star   wish   far
shed   well   that

Activity 7

for   for   for   for

10   Activity Book B

Name _____

Lesson 49
_____

ch

Activity 1

ch ch ch ch ch
ch ch ch ch ch

Activity 3

sick   wish   sack   lets
lift   star   ten   help

Activity 6

Gramps   stops   this
band   smart   wish

Activity Book B   11

Name _____

Lesson 49
Activity 7

you This have was said

1. **This** is a pig.

2. Ren **said**, "Fix the top."

3. The cats **have** a big box.

4. The frog **was** in the pond.

5. Can **you** dig a pit?

says   says   **says**

12   Activity Book B

Answer Key Activity Book B   19

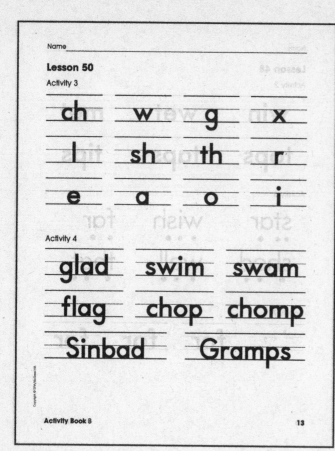
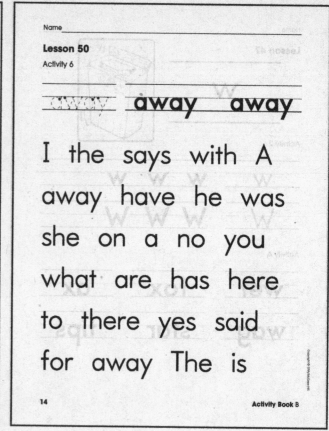
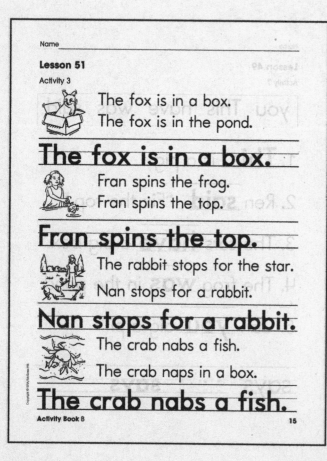
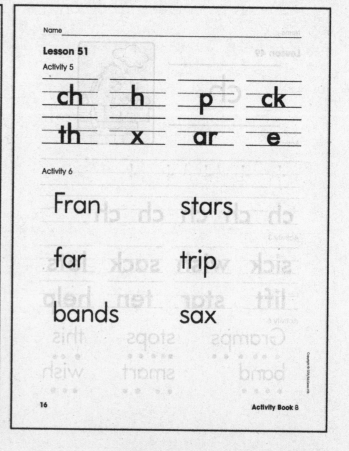

Name

Lesson 50
Activity 3

ch	w	g	x
l	sh	th	r
e	a	o	i

Activity 4

glad	swim	swam
flag	chop	chomp
Sinbad		Gramps

Name

Lesson 50
Activity 6

~~away~~   away   away

I the says with A
away have he was
she on a no you
what are has here
to there yes said
for away The is

Name

Lesson 51
Activity 3

The fox is in a box.
The fox is in the pond.

The fox is in a box.

Fran spins the frog.
Fran spins the top.

Fran spins the top.

The rabbit stops for the star.
Nan stops for a rabbit.

Nan stops for a rabbit.

The crab nabs a fish.
The crab naps in a box.

The crab nabs a fish.

Name

Lesson 51
Activity 5

ch	h	p	ck
th	x	ar	e

Activity 6

Fran	stars
far	trip
bands	sax

Lesson 51

Activity 8

1. The frog hops fast.

2. Ron spins the top.

3. Mom can fix the car.

4. The raft is in the pond.

5. Tom can start the car.

6. The pigs are in the barn.

7. Pam sat in the grass.

8. The top is off the box.

9. The frogs hop in the pond.

Lesson 52

Activity 3

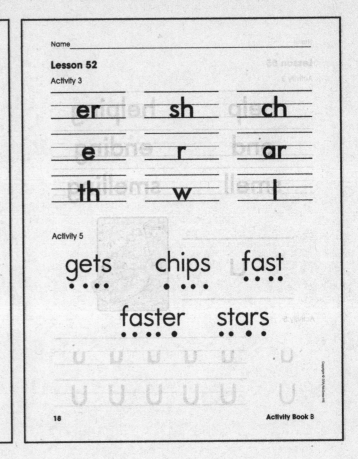

er   sh   ch

e   r   ar

th   w   l

Activity 5

gets   chips   fast

faster   stars

Lesson 53

Activity 2

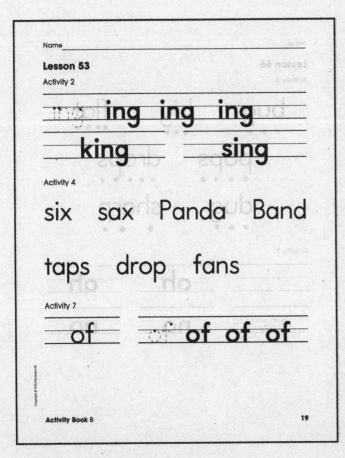

ing   ing   ing

king   sing

Activity 4

six   sax   Panda   Band

taps   drop   fans

Activity 7

of   of   of of of

Lesson 54

Activity 2

ring   bring

helping   ending

Activity 5

mops   stops   this

can't   drips

spots   tots   band

tops   hand

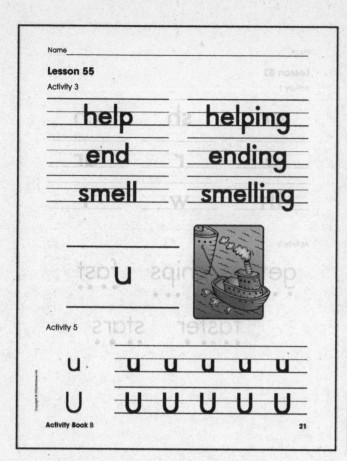

Lesson 55

Activity 3

help   helping

end   ending

smell   smelling

—— u ——

Activity 5

u   U U U U U U

U   U U U U U U

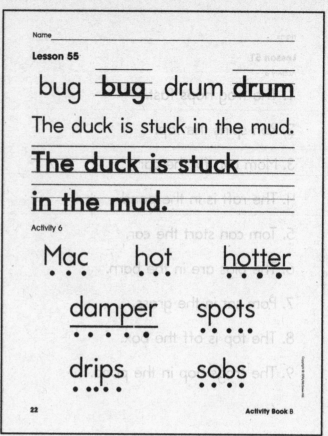

bug **bug** drum **drum**

The duck is stuck in the mud.

The duck is stuck

in the mud.

Activity 6

Mac   hot   hotter

damper   spots

drips   sobs

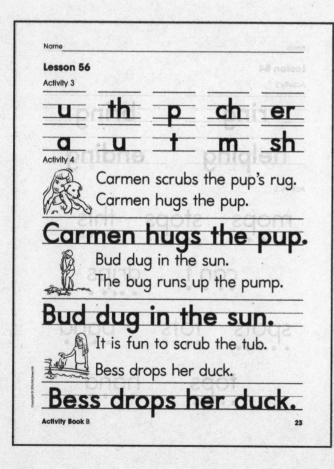

Lesson 56

Activity 3

u   th   p   ch   er

a   u   t   m   sh

Activity 4

Carmen scrubs the pup's rug.
Carmen hugs the pup.

Carmen hugs the pup.

Bud dug in the sun.
The bug runs up the pump.

Bud dug in the sun.

It is fun to scrub the tub.
Bess drops her duck.

Bess drops her duck.

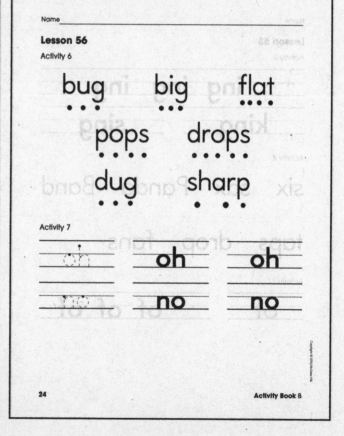

Lesson 56

Activity 6

bug   big   flat

pops   drops

dug   sharp

Activity 7

——   oh   oh

——   no   no

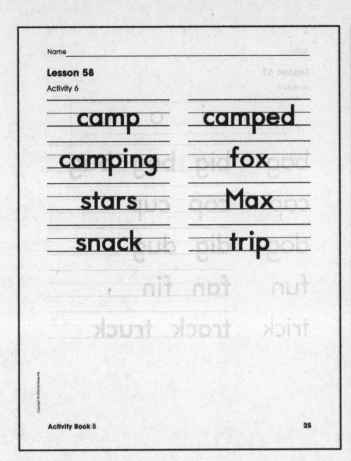

Lesson 58

Activity 6

<u>camp</u>   <u>camped</u>

<u>camping</u>   <u>fox</u>

<u>stars</u>   <u>Max</u>

<u>snack</u>   <u>trip</u>

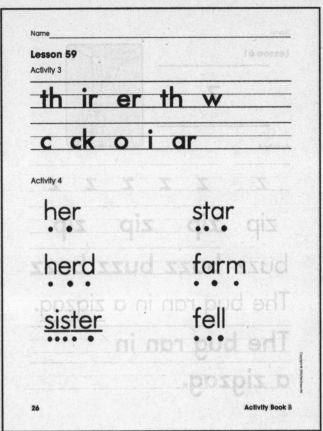

Lesson 59

Activity 3

th ir er th w

c ck o i ar

Activity 4

<u>her</u>   <u>star</u>
.•.   ..•.

<u>herd</u>   <u>farm</u>
.•.   .•.

<u>sister</u>   <u>fell</u>
••.•.•   .••.

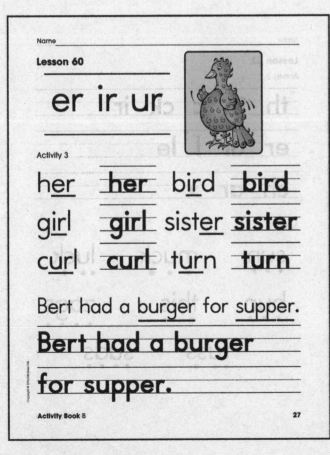

Lesson 60

er ir ur

Activity 3

h<u>er</u> <u>her</u> b<u>ir</u>d <u>bird</u>

g<u>ir</u>l <u>girl</u> sist<u>er</u> <u>sister</u>

c<u>ur</u>l <u>curl</u> t<u>ur</u>n <u>turn</u>

Bert had a <u>burger</u> for <u>supper</u>.

<u>**Bert had a burger**</u>

<u>**for supper.**</u>

Lesson 60

Activity 4

<u>nest</u>   <u>with</u>

<u>packed</u>   <u>camping</u>

<u>mix</u>   <u>mixer</u>

<u>sister</u>   <u>mother</u>

<u>bird</u>

Activity 6

have is oh a of the as on

she he has for was says with

here to you are what there

yes said away The no but I

Name

Lesson 61

Activity 4

Z

z z z z z z

zip **zip zip zip**

buzz **buzz buzz buzz**

The bug ran in a zigzag.

The bug ran in

a zigzag.

Name

Lesson 61

Activity 6

a	i	o	u

bag **big bog bug**

cap **cop cup**

dog **dig dug**

fun **fan fin**

trick **track truck**

Name

Lesson 61

Activity 8

packed   camped
͏. . . . .
tramped   tracked
. . . .

fixed
. . . . .

Name

Lesson 62

Activity 2

th th c ck ir

er ur l le

ch ar x

Activity 3

sun   muck   luck
. . .   .
bun   this   zags
. . .   .

fuss   suds
. . . .

Name

Lesson 62

Activity 5

does   **does**   **does**

one   **one**   **one**

Name

Lesson 63

y

Activity 4

y   y y y y y

yam **yam** yes **yes**

yell **yell** yet **yet**

Name

Lesson 63

Activity 5

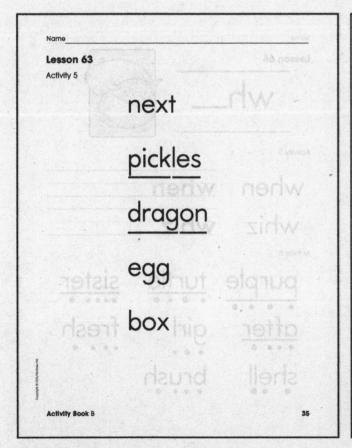

next

pickles

dragon

egg

box

Name

Lesson 63

Activity 6

The dog yelps _____ at the rabbit.

A rabbit nibbles in the yard.

The dog naps in the yard.

Answer Key Activity Book B   **25**

Lesson 64
Activity 2

ch sh th th y

ir er ur x z

Activity 3

with   yelps   yards

birds   Zack

nibble   backyard

runners   wiggle

Lesson 64
Activity 4

does	has	was
one	have	is
his	he	here

one = 1
two = 2
three = 3

two   two two two

three   three

one two three

Lesson 64
Activity 6

The dog yelps at the rabbit.
A rabbit nibbles in the yard.
The dog naps in the yard.

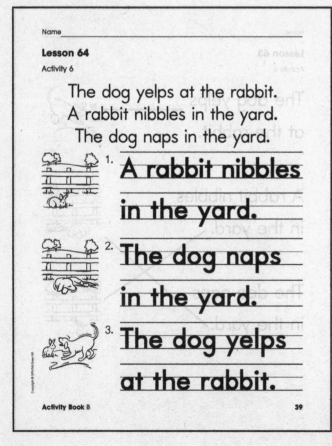

1. **A rabbit nibbles in the yard.**

2. **The dog naps in the yard.**

3. **The dog yelps at the rabbit.**

Lesson 65

wh___

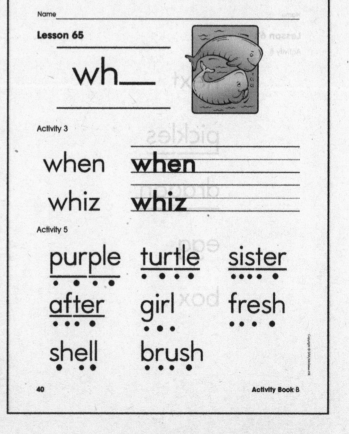

Activity 3

when   **when**

whiz   **whiz**

Activity 5

purple   turtle   sister

after   girl   fresh

shell   brush

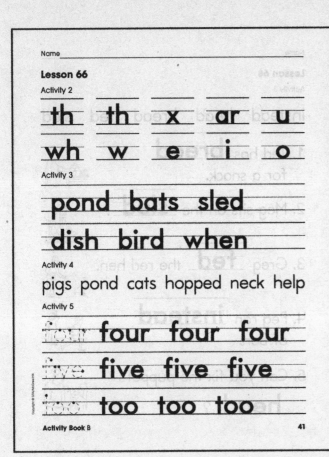

Name _____

Lesson 66

Activity 2

| th | th | x | ar | u |
| wh | w | e | i | o |

Activity 3

pond bats sled

dish bird when

Activity 4

pigs pond cats hopped neck help

Activity 5

four four four four

five five five five

too too too too

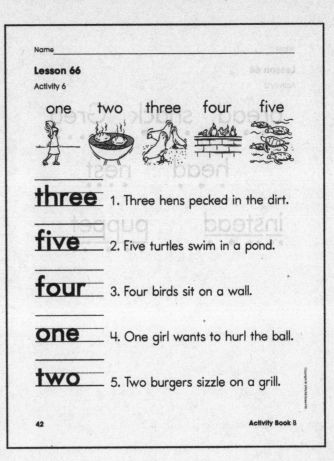

Name _____

Lesson 66

Activity 6

one   two   three   four   five

three   1. Three hens pecked in the dirt.

five   2. Five turtles swim in a pond.

four   3. Four birds sit on a wall.

one   4. One girl wants to hurl the ball.

two   5. Two burgers sizzle on a grill.

Name _____

Lesson 67

Activity 1

| One | Two | Three | Four | Five |

Three hens pecked in the dirt.

Five turtles swim in a pond.

Four birds sit on a wall.

One girl wants to hurl the ball.

Two burgers sizzle on a grill.

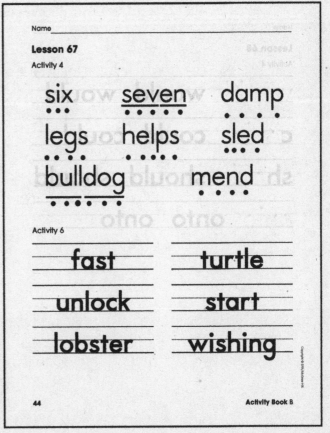

Name _____

Lesson 67

Activity 4

six   seven   damp

legs   helps   sled

bulldog   mend

Activity 6

fast   turtle

unlock   start

lobster   wishing

Name

Lesson 68
Activity 2

bread　　snack　　Greg
•••　　••••　　•••

head　　　nest
•••　　　•••

in<u>stead</u>　　<u>pupp</u>et
•••••　　　•••

Name

Lesson 68
Activity 3

<u>instead</u>　<u>head</u>　<u>bread</u>　<u>fed</u>　<u>sled</u>

1. Ted has **bread**
   for a snack.

2. Meg sits on the **sled**.

3. Greg **fed** the red hen.

4. Peg ran **instead**
   of Ben.

5. Can you fix the puppet's
   head?

Name

Lesson 68
Activity 4

would　would
could　could
should　should
onto　onto

Name

Lesson 69
Activity 1

r　　ir　　er
ur　　th　　th
z　　i　　e
ea　　w　　wh

Activity 2

ai　　ai　　ai
al　　al　　al
all　　all　　all

c<u>all</u>　b<u>all</u>　sm<u>all</u>

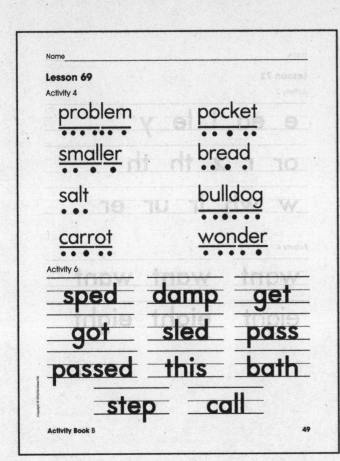
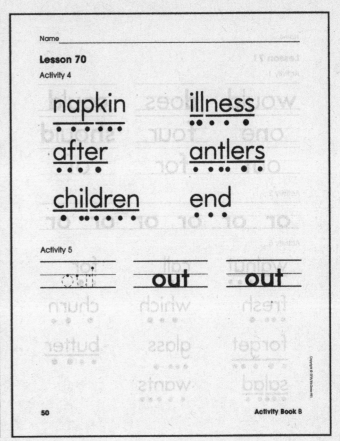

Name_____

Lesson 69

Activity 4

problem   pocket

smaller   bread

salt   bulldog

carrot   wonder

Activity 6

sped	damp	get
got	sled	pass
passed	this	bath
	step	call

Name_____

Lesson 70

Activity 4

napkin   illness

after   antlers

children   end

Activity 5

| | out | out |

Name_____

Lesson 70

Activity 5

the I have is A on she

he was with as to you

here what there The for

says too away one me has his

would two five my onto

should four could three does

a Is are no but

oh no out of said where

Name_____

Lesson 70

Activity 6

| napkin | illness | antlers |
| children | end | after |

1. His **illness** had him in bed.

2. The **children** have fun with blocks.

3. The animal's **antlers** are big.

4. Do you have a **napkin** for supper?

5. Let's run to the **end** of the block.

6. The dog ran **after** the cat.

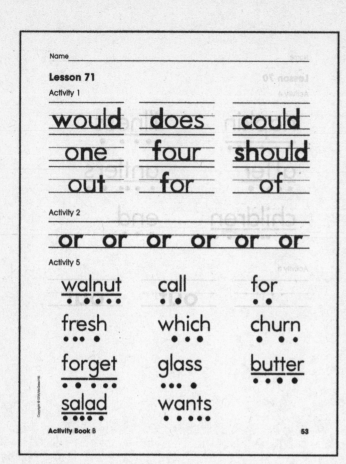
Lesson 71
Activity 1

would   does   could

one   four   should

out   for   of

Activity 2

or   or   or   or   or   or

Activity 5

walnut   call   for

fresh   which   churn

forget   glass   butter

salad   wants

Activity Book B   53

Lesson 72
Activity 2

e   ea   l   le   y

or   r   z   th   th

w   wh   ir   ur   er

Activity 4

want   want   want

eight   eight   eight

54   **Activity Book** B

Lesson 72
Activity 5

animals   Wendell

lots   class

lizard   wonderful

whir   problem

paddle   salad

Activity Book B   55

Lesson 73

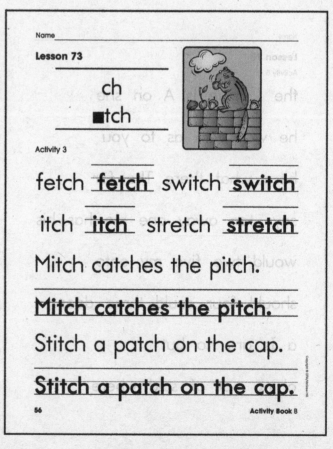

ch
■tch

Activity 3

fetch **fetch** switch **switch**

itch **itch** stretch **stretch**

Mitch catches the pitch.

Mitch catches the pitch.

Stitch a patch on the cap.

Stitch a patch on the cap.

56   **Activity Book** B

---

30   **Answer Key** Activity Book B

Lesson 73

Activity 6

<u>Wendell</u> went swam

frog next step

<u>stepped</u> grab <u>grabbed</u>

<u>dipped</u> slip <u>slipped</u>

<u>landed</u> <u>bottom</u> fell

Lesson 74

Activity 3

pinch ⟶ pinched ⟶ pinching

shop ⟶ shopped ⟶ shopping

want ⟶ wanted ⟶ wanting

step ⟶ stepped ⟶ stepping

hand ⟶ handed ⟶ handing

Activity 4

which will match
• • • • • • • •

when then next
• • • • • • • • • •

wetter lizard class
• • • • •• • • ••• •

Lesson 74

Activity 5

pull pull **pull pull**

put put **put put**

<u>where</u> <u>want</u> <u>out</u>

<u>here</u> <u>of</u> <u>has</u>

<u>is</u> <u>are</u>

Lesson 75

k
c
■ck

Activity 4

k **k** **k** **k** **k** **k**

kick <u>**kick**</u> bark <u>**bark**</u>

kitchen <u>**kitchen**</u> silk <u>**silk**</u>

The kitten laps milk.

<u>**The kitten laps milk.**</u>

Name

Lesson 75
Activity 6

Wendell lizard

Allen when

duck puts

class pets

frogs glad

bugs went

Name

Lesson 76
Activity 4

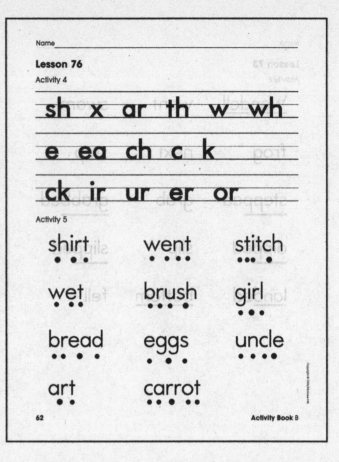

sh x ar th w wh

e ea ch c k

ck ir ur er or

Activity 5

shirt went stitch

wet brush girl

bread eggs uncle

art carrot

Name

Lesson 76
Activity 6

there where here

could would should

want of you

pull put

Name

Lesson 76
Activity 7

1. Sherman has six shells in a box.

2. This is a thin twig.

3. Stitch a patch on the cap.

4. Ellen hit the ball with her tennis racket.

5. The rabbit got away from the fox.

6. Sam had bread and butter.

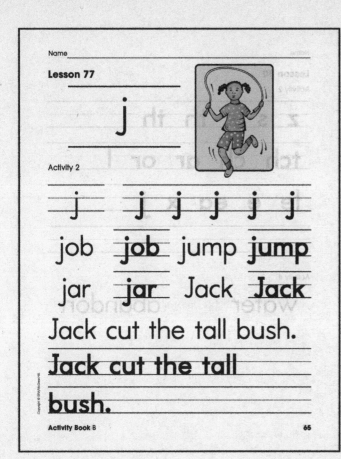

Lesson 77

Activity 2

j

job job jump jump

jar jar Jack Jack

Jack cut the tall bush.

Jack cut the tall bush.

Lesson 77

Activity 4

uncle	salt	mixer
stir	little	bread
butter	milk	carrots
nuts	whir	batter

Activity 5

glass	milk
Art	turned
mixer	that
handed	butter
	batter

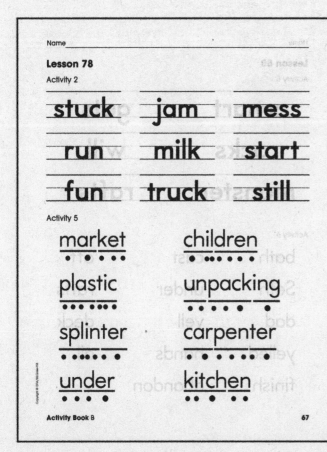

Lesson 78

Activity 2

stuck	jam	mess
run	milk	start
fun	truck	still

Activity 5

market   children

plastic   unpacking

splinter   carpenter

under   kitchen

Lesson 78

Activity 7

| strip   splash   splinter   scratches |

1. The frog jumped into the pond with a **splash**.

2. Max has a **splinter** in his hand.

3. The carpenter cut a thin **strip** of plastic.

4. The dog **scratches** its chin.

Lesson 79
Activity 5

hen	flap	pen
past	call	this
bed	fell	head
called	mend	run
flapped		

Lesson 80
Activity 2

z s s th th

tch ch ar or l

le e ea x j

Activity 4

water   abandon

Lesson 80
Activity 4

want eight my when

there have I a the

on she he was with what

here to you said for

pull says too away one

me two onto should four

could three would does

five The are A no but

oh no out of put where

hurray water abandon

Lesson 80
Activity 5

smart	gets
rocks	will
monster	rafts

Activity 6

bath	cast	off
Seth	under	rafts
dad	yell	deck
yelled	hands	all
finish	abandon	

hitter   dishes

called   Chuck

ball   catcher

Activity 6

be   be   be   be

do   do   do   do

---

crutches

sandwich

kitchen

under

understand

glitter

---

dishes   plastic   fishnet

carpet   splinter   carpenter

garden   boxes.

Activity 4

Patches and Dan

1. Dan pitches the stick.

2. Patches wants to catch it.

3. The stick splashes into the pond.

4. Patches fetches the stick.

3   4   2   1

---

dge

fudge   fudge

edge   edge

judge   judge

badge   badge

Top Left Panel

Name _____

Lesson 81
Activity 4

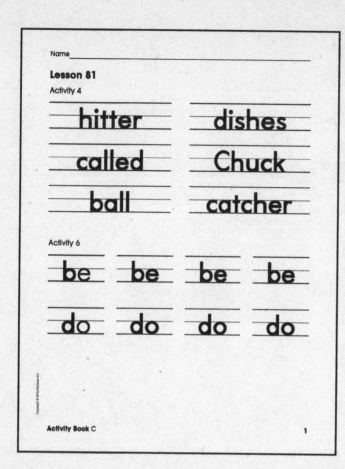

hitter   dishes
called   Chuck
ball   catcher

Activity 6

be be be be
do do do do

Activity Book C   1

Top Right Panel

Name _____

Lesson 82
Activity 4

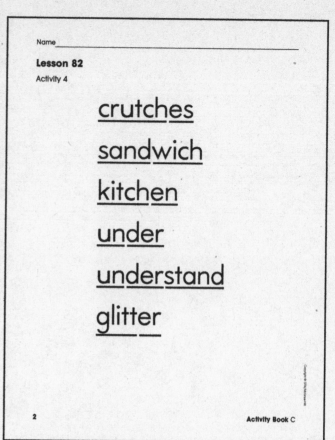

crutches
sandwich
kitchen
under
understand
glitter

2   **Activity Book** C

Bottom Left Panel

Name _____

Lesson 83
Activity 3

dishes   plastic   fishnet
carpet   splinter   carpenter
garden   boxes

Activity 4

Patches and Dan

1. Dan pitches the stick.
2. Patches wants to catch it.
3. The stick splashes into the pond.
4. Patches fetches the stick.

3   2   4   1

Activity Book C   3

Bottom Right Panel

Name _____

Lesson 83
Activity 5

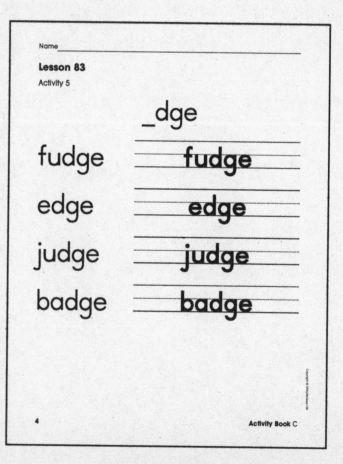

_dge

fudge   fudge
edge   edge
judge   judge
badge   badge

4   **Activity Book** C

Lesson 83

Activity 6

trash   drum   flag

stash   split   then

bench   scrap   lunch

children   garden

fishnet   dented

Activity 7

half   three   five

two   four   one

Activity Book C   5

Lesson 84

Activity 2

clam   made

helps   club

swam   insect

lake   plane

Activity 3

w   wh   ch   tch   p

j   _dge   th   th   r

sh   x   ir   ur   er

6   **Activity Book** C

Lesson 84

Activity 5

market   cannot

wishes   nickel

garden   chicken

Activity 6

I'm   I'm   I'm

today   today   today

Activity Book C   7

Lesson 85

Activity 1

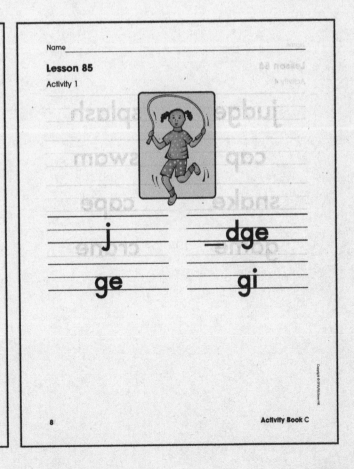

j   _dge

ge   gi

8   **Activity Book** C

Lesson 85
Activity 3

_dge a_e p k ea

j or al f h e

wh y le z ur u

r ing er ch w l

tch th x c ar ck

b sh o g ir c r

Activity Book C

9

Lesson 85
Activity 6

lamp   lad   first

back   with   costs

sell   full   <u>asked</u>

scratch <u>nickel</u> <u>scratched</u>

Activity 7

of said do

have today be

we he she does

10

Activity Book C

Lesson 86
Activity 4

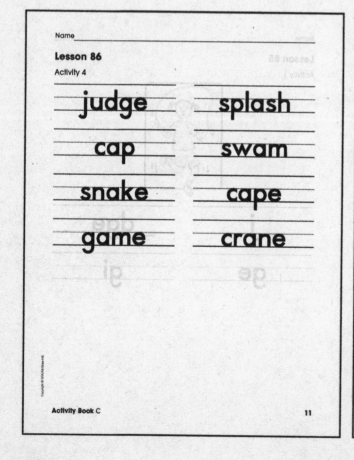

judge   splash

cap   swam

snake   cape

game   crane

Activity Book C

11

Lesson 86
Activity 5

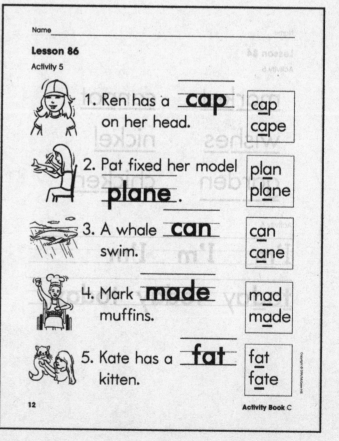

1. Ren has a **cap** on her head.   cap / c<u>a</u>pe

2. Pat fixed her model **plane**.   plan / pl<u>a</u>ne

3. A whale **can** swim.   can / c<u>a</u>ne

4. Mark **made** muffins.   m<u>a</u>d / m<u>a</u>de

5. Kate has a **fat** kitten.   fat / f<u>a</u>te

12

Activity Book C

38

Answer Key Activity Book C

Lesson 86
Activity 6

<u>they</u>   <u>they</u>   <u>they</u>

<u>were</u>   <u>were</u>   <u>were</u>

Activity 7

<u>c</u>alled	wat<u>ch</u>	lake
snake	<u>sh</u>ade	wade
awake	waded	mistake
fi<u>sh</u>	<u>sh</u>ape	thin<u>g</u>s
crossed		

Activity Book C

13

Lesson 87
Activity 2

sn<u>a</u>ke	mad
cr<u>a</u>ne	made
h<u>i</u>de	rip
<u>a</u>ge	ripe
p<u>a</u>ge	Tim
c<u>a</u>ke	time

Activity 3

ee

m<u>ee</u>t	f<u>ee</u>t	k<u>ee</u>p
sl<u>ee</u>p	wh<u>ee</u>l	b<u>ee</u>
j<u>ee</u>p	thr<u>ee</u>	s<u>ee</u>
sh<u>ee</u>p	f<u>ee</u>l	w<u>ee</u>d

14   **Activity Book** C

Lesson 87

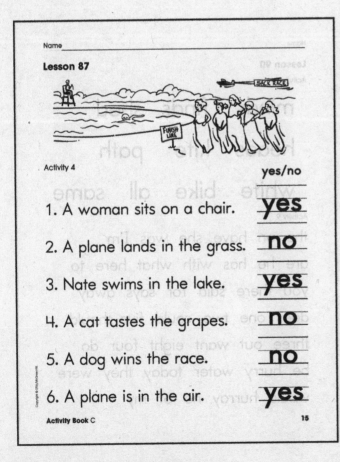

Activity 4

                                        yes/no

1. A woman sits on a chair.   **yes**

2. A plane lands in the grass.   **no**

3. Nate swims in the lake.   **yes**

4. A cat tastes the grapes.   **no**

5. A dog wins the race.   **no**

6. A plane is in the air.   **yes**

Activity Book C   15

Lesson 88
Activity 2

J<u>a</u>ne	j<u>a</u>r	t<u>i</u>de
j<u>a</u>bbed	t<u>a</u>ke	n<u>i</u>ne
ri<u>dge</u>	j<u>e</u>t	li<u>ttle</u>
ba<u>ck</u>	d<u>i</u>me	<u>g</u>entle

Activity 3

s<u>eat</u>	<u>each</u>	<u>eat</u>
m<u>eat</u>	b<u>each</u>	
b<u>ean</u>s	<u>eagle</u>	

16   **Activity Book** C

Answer Key Activity Book C

Lesson 88
Activity 4

under   finish

escape   gigantic

kitchen   milkshake

Activity 5

sick   eggs

cake   little

fudge   like

Lesson 89
Activity 2

j ge gi _dge

c k ck w wh ir er ur

e ea z s ee ea tch ch

Activity 5

when   trip   page
cape   hunt   large

Activity 6

magic   battle   blazes
escape   camels   giraffes

Lesson 90
Activity 2

hide   hid

fine   fin

rid   slid

slide   ride

Activity 3

parade   inside

Emma   April

Kamara   wagon

Lesson 90
Activity 7

minds   finds   shed

heads   kite   path

white   bike   all   same

Activity 9

the on have she was I'm
are he has with what here to
you there said for says away
does one two could five should
three out want eight four do
be hurry water today they were
would hurray no of my

Name

Lesson 91

s
ce
ci

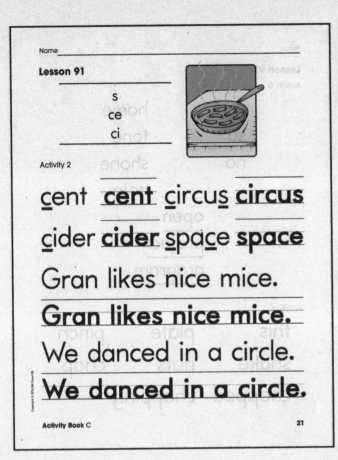

Activity 2

c̲ent **c̲ent** c̲ircu̲s **c̲ircu̲s**

c̲ider **c̲ider** spa̲c̲e **spa̲c̲e**

Gran likes nice mice.

Gran likes nice mice.

We danced in a circle.

We danced in a circle.

Activity Book C   21

Name

Lesson 91

Activity 3

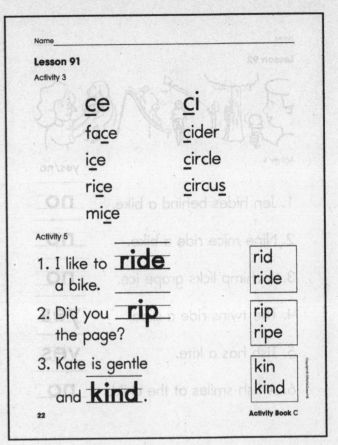

c̲e	c̲i
fac̲e	c̲ider
ic̲e	c̲ircle
ric̲e	c̲ircu̲s
mic̲e	

Activity 5

1. I like to **ride**
   a bike. _____

2. Did you **rip**
   the page?

3. Kate is gentle
   and **kind**.

| rid |
| ride |

| rip |
| ripe |

| kin |
| kind |

22   Activity Book C

Name

Lesson 91

Activity 7

f̲i̲ne   sm̲i̲les   k̲i̲te

para̲de   s̲a̲ved   r̲i̲des

tr̲i̲ke   sh̲e̲d   a̲fter

bridge   head   sp̲i̲ke

wh̲i̲ne   l̲a̲ke   h̲i̲m

Activity Book C   23

Name

Lesson 92

Activity 3

twins	**spine**
tree	**nine**
ten	**slide**
time	**slim**

Activity 5

pl̲a̲te	n̲u̲t	ch̲o̲p	d̲a̲te
n̲i̲ne	shak̲e	p̲i̲nch	that
sli̲ce	ri̲pe	spi̲ce	c̲a̲ke

24   Activity Book C

Name

Lesson 92

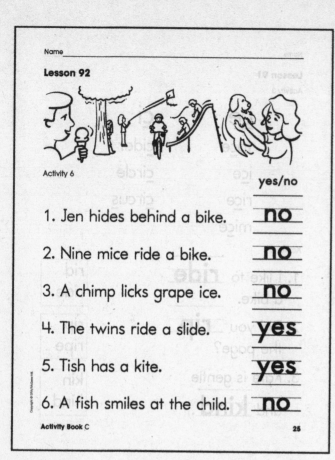

Activity 6

yes/no

1. Jen hides behind a bike.   **no**

2. Nine mice ride a bike.   **no**

3. A chimp licks grape ice.   **no**

4. The twins ride a slide.   **yes**

5. Tish has a kite.   **yes**

6. A fish smiles at the child.   **no**

Activity Book C   25

Name

Lesson 93

Activity 3

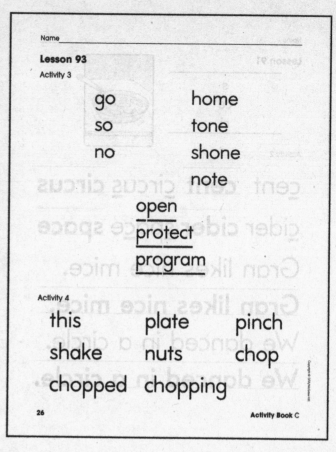

go	home
so	tone
no	shone
	note

open

protect

program

Activity 4

this	plate	pinch
shake	nuts	chop
chopped	chopping	

26   **Activity Book** C

Name

Lesson 93

Activity 5

make	spice	save
can	taste	and
slice	stir	then
like	while	nice
ripe	help	date

Activity Book C   27

Name

Lesson 94

Activity 2

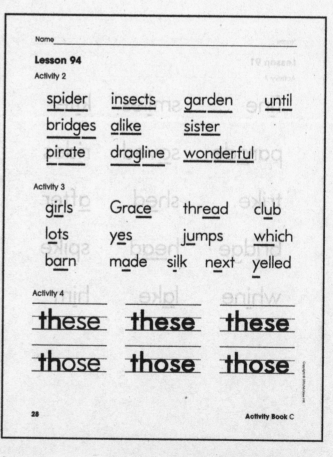

spider	insects	garden	until
bridges	alike	sister	
pirate	dragline	wonderful	

Activity 3

girls	Grace	thread	club
lots	yes	jumps	which
barn	made	silk	next	yelled

Activity 4

these	these	these
those	those	those

28   **Activity Book** C

Answer Key Activity Book C

Lesson 95

Activity 1

ur	ce	s	ck	ir
gi	ci	i_e	ea	ee
ge	a_e	al	or	y
ch	le	tch	_dge	o_e

Activity 3

where	one	two
four	eight	what
here	out	his
were	my	said

Lesson 95

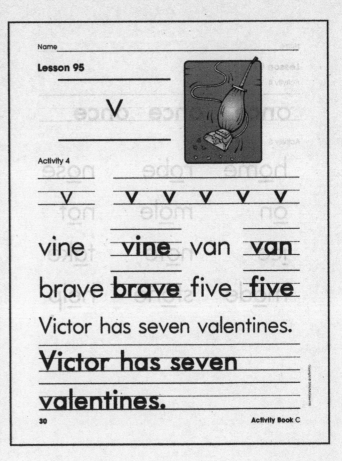

V

Activity 4

V   V V V V V

vine   **vine**   van   **van**

brave   **brave**   five   **five**

Victor has seven valentines.

Victor has seven valentines.

Lesson 95

Activity 4

van	vet
silver	drive
seven	visit
never	vase

Lesson 97

Activity 1

ol	v	o_e	ce	ol
a_e	j	r	f	d
gi	ar	ck	sh	tch
ing	ir	th	o_e	ol

Activity 2

cold	home
snug	stone
hello	ice
frozen	stove

Lesson 97
Activity 4

<u>o</u>nce   <u>o</u>nce   once

Activity 5

h<u>o</u>me   r<u>o</u>be   n<u>o</u>se

<u>o</u>n   m<u>o</u>le   n<u>o</u>t

<u>i</u>ce   n<u>o</u>te   t<u>a</u>ke

m<u>a</u>de   st<u>o</u>ne   h<u>e</u>lp

Lesson 98
Activity 2

<u>**surprise**</u>   <u>**perfect**</u>

<u>**suppose**</u>   <u>**problem**</u>

<u>**solved**</u>   <u>**closed**</u>

Activity 5

<u>problem</u>   <u>perfect</u>

<u>forest</u>   <u>suppose</u>

<u>outside</u>   <u>baskets</u>

<u>pocket</u>   <u>acorn</u>

<u>secret</u>

Lesson 99
Activity 3

be   pet   she   we

cold   bugs   me   red

will   stone   shade   for

Activity 4

huge   bu<u>g</u>s   m<u>u</u>le   pipe

tr<u>a</u>de   tr<u>a</u>des   tr<u>a</u>der

bran<u>ch</u>   bran<u>ch</u>es   bud<u>g</u>e

<u>u</u>se   <u>u</u>sed   pu<u>sh</u>

Lesson 99
Activity 5

<u>secret</u>   <u>refuse</u>

<u>forest</u>   <u>music</u>

<u>river</u>   <u>animals</u>

<u>Alfonso</u>   <u>amuse</u>

<u>Amazon</u>   <u>baskets</u>

<u>Cupid</u>

Name_____

Lesson 100
Activity 1

sh	ar	or	ch
tch	j	_dge	ge
gi	s	ce	ci
lo	al	all	e
ea	v	z	s

Name_____

Lesson 100
Activity 4

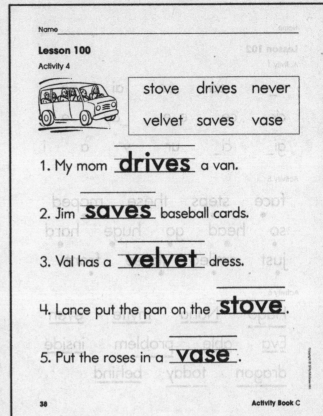

stove	drives	never
velvet	saves	vase

1. My mom **drives** a van.

2. Jim **saves** baseball cards.

3. Val has a **velvet** dress.

4. Lance put the pan on the **stove**.

5. Put the roses in a **vase**.

Name_____

Lesson 100
Activity 7

have onto was today

I'm are what does

here to you there my

said oh says away of

one two could should

three out want eight

four do half hurry water

they were would hurray

those once wrote these

oh no where pull put

Name_____

Lesson 101
Activity 4

<u>s</u>ecret   pocke<u>t</u>

<u>a</u>corn   dragon

dragon<u>s</u>   terrible

tickl<u>ed</u>   <u>li</u>ttle

<u>e</u>ven   fever

Lesson 102

Activity 1

a_e   ea   ee   ai   ge

ck   ce   e_e   _ay   e

gi_   ci_   ur   y   a   i

Activity 5

face   steps   these   moped

so   head   go   huge   hard

just   smiled   those   front

Activity 6

Hugo   Nana   invite   even

Eva   able   problem   inside

dragon   today   behind

Lesson 103

Activity 2

● The giraffe has a long neck.

○ Eve runs from the giraffe.

○ The man is on skates.

● The man is on a trapeze.

○ We sat on the fence.

● We put a dime in the meter.

Lesson 103

Activity 3

qu   qu   qu   qu   qu   qu

Activity 5

huge   pole

inside   held

itch   bugs

next   quick

Lesson 104

Activity 1

eat   mail   dream   colds   better

Sunday   creak   cheek   tickle   speak

tea   feel   quick   shark   pals

Activity 2

dragons   terrible   sneezing

quiet   maintain

ankle   player

Activity 3

see   since   creak

sneeze   fever   flame

Lesson 105

Activity 2

q<u>u</u>een   sq<u>u</u>id   s<u>ea</u>

f<u>ea</u>st   m<u>ea</u>l   sq<u>u</u>eal

h<u>u</u>ge   l<u>iqu</u>id   awa<u>y</u>

Lesson 106

Activity 1

ci   qu   ai   qu   ce   ay

ear   ing   tch   ai   z   qu

gi   a_e   ee   u   qu   ay

ci   sh   th   ce   ai   qu

Activity 2

sea   **queen**

squid   **feast**

squint   **squeal**

squirted   **time**

Lesson 106

Activity 5

dr<u>ea</u>m   d<u>uck</u>   gr<u>ee</u>n

und<u>er</u>   l<u>ea</u>ves   sa<u>v</u>ed

<u>sh</u>ark   s<u>ea</u>   sq<u>u</u>id

qu<u>i</u>te   <u>qu</u>it   h<u>uge</u>

fa<u>ce</u>   asl<u>ee</u>p

<u>d</u>ark   hurra<u>y</u>

Lesson 107

Activity 1

ee   ear   ay   ai   qu

i_e   eer   ay   qu   _y

ge   ur   eer   ear   u_e

y   ai   er   ir   ce

Activity 3

m<u>ai</u>l   <u>qu</u>ack   rep<u>ea</u>t

<u>b</u>arked   dr<u>ea</u>ms   stor<u>y</u>

fl<u>ea</u>s   bees   ne<u>x</u>t

chase   awa<u>y</u>   <u>sh</u>eep

little   <u>h</u>ear   h<u>u</u>rry

Lesson 107

Activity 4

s<u>o</u>me   <u>some   some</u>

<u>y</u>our   <u>your your</u>

Activity 5

s<u>ai</u>l   d<u>ay</u>   F<u>ay</u>

R<u>ay</u>   b<u>ai</u>l   r<u>ai</u>n

toda<u>y</u>   w<u>ai</u>t   m<u>ai</u>n

b<u>ai</u>t   afr<u>ai</u>d   st<u>ay</u>

r<u>ai</u>se   s<u>ai</u>ling

Lesson 108

Activity 4

dr<u>ea</u>ms   <u>Qu</u>incy   qu<u>ack</u>

<u>qu</u>acked   rep<u>ea</u>t   h<u>urr</u>y

sp<u>o</u>ke   sl<u>ee</u>p   w<u>a</u>ke

<u>three</u>   stor<u>y</u>   st<u>or</u>ies

<u>l</u>eaves   fl<u>ea</u>s   t<u>i</u>red

Lesson 109

Activity 1

ear   ur   y_   qu   a_e

ai   ge   ci   z   ee

_dge   a_e   v   ol   al

tch   r   i   a   e_e

Activity 4

<u>dreamers</u>   dreaming   <u>Quincy</u>

duckling   opossum   <u>table</u>

napkins   puppies   every

<u>invited</u>   begins   <u>ribbons</u>

Lesson 110

Activity 1

ci   ch   ck   ce   c

ai   _are _y   sh   o_e

qu   _ay   ee   ce   c

gi   al   d   b   u_e

tch   th   r   ur   ir

Activity 2

<u>west</u>   <u>may</u>   <u>mayor</u>

<u>table</u>   <u>over</u>   <u>hero</u>

<u>carry</u>   <u>ribbon</u>   <u>stick</u>

<u>ice</u>

Lesson 110
Activity 3

scare	squirrel	umpire	store
deer	more	scored	square

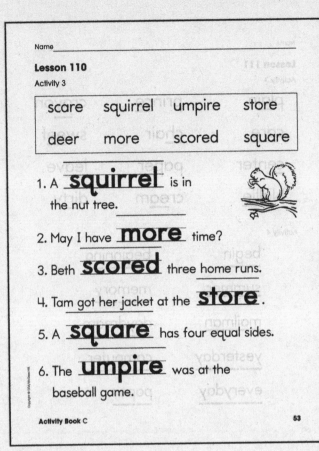

1. A **squirrel** is in the nut tree.
2. May I have **more** time?
3. Beth **scored** three home runs.
4. Tam got her jacket at the **store**.
5. A **square** has four equal sides.
6. The **umpire** was at the baseball game.

Activity Book C   53

Lesson 110
Activity 5

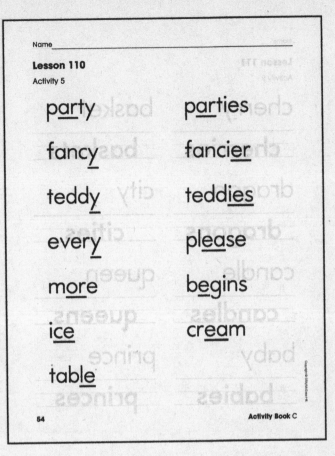

p<u>ar</u>ty	p<u>ar</u>ties
fanc<u>y</u>	fanci<u>er</u>
tedd<u>y</u>	tedd<u>ies</u>
ever<u>y</u>	pl<u>ea</u>se
m<u>or</u>e	b<u>e</u>gins
<u>ic</u>e	cr<u>ea</u>m
tab<u>le</u>	

54   Activity Book C

Lesson 110
Activity 6

Oh   half   Mr.   where
pull   was   are   have
Mrs.   here   what   to
you   there   put   said   those
says   away   of   does   one
two   wrote   could   onto   would
out   four   want   eight   should
oh   no   hurry   my   water
do   I'm   these   today
they   were   once   heard   some
your   bear

Activity Book C   55

Lesson 111

i
_igh
i_e

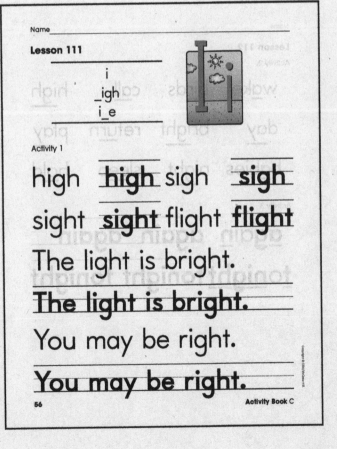

Activity 1

high **high** sigh **sigh**
sight **sight** flight **flight**
The light is bright.
The light is bright.
You may be right.
You may be right.

56   Activity Book C

Answer Key Activity Book C

49

Lesson 111
Activity 2

cherry	basket
cherries	**baskets**
dragon	city
dragons	**cities**
candle	queen
candles	**queens**
baby	prince
babies	**princes**

Activity Book C 57

Lesson 111
Activity 3

pla<u>i</u>n	prin<u>ce</u>	<u>cr</u>ayon
ca<u>re</u>	<u>ch</u>air	sw<u>ee</u>t
<u>c</u>enter	paper	leav<u>e</u>
Nelli<u>e</u>	cr<u>ea</u>m	d<u>ir</u>ty

Activity 4

begin	beginning
<u>summer</u>	memory
<u>mailman</u>	daydream
yesterday	computer
everyday	paper

58 **Activity Book** C

Lesson 112
Activity 2

w<u>a</u>ke	b<u>ir</u>ds	c<u>all</u>	h<u>igh</u>
day	bright	retur<u>n</u>	pla<u>y</u>
b<u>a</u>bies	night	sleep	hold

Activity 3

<u>ag</u>ain <u>ag</u>ain <u>ag</u>ain

to<u>night</u> to<u>night</u> to<u>night</u>

Activity Book C 59

Lesson 112
Activity 4

<u>returns</u>	tonight	<u>babies</u>
opossum	beginner	<u>insects</u>
daylight	<u>thunder</u>	frighten
lightbulb	high chair	spider

Activity 5

five	**light**
freeze	**plays**
holding	**sleeps**
night	**insect**

60 **Activity Book** C

50

Answer Key Activity Book C

Lesson 112
Activity 7

1. See the **deer** run.

deer
dean

2. Mom **rakes** leaves.

racks
rakes

3. A whale swims in the **sea**.

sea
seal

4. I eat **meat** for dinner.

meat
mean

5. The dog does a **flip**.

flea
flip

Lesson 113
Activity 3

fly	tie	tries	pie	sky

1. The **fly** buzzes on my head.

2. I made the cherry **pie** by myself.

3. Spot **tries** to do a trick.

Activity 4

rained	night	paint	high
swing	children	better	eagle
returning	wake	birds	shine
city	snail	afraid	letters

Lesson 113
Activity 5

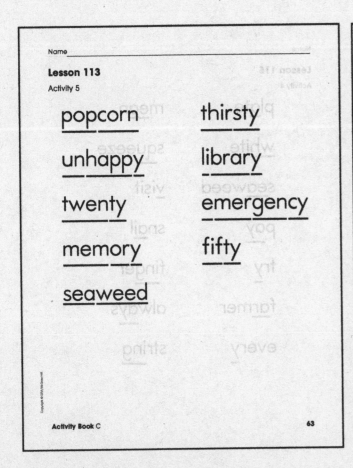

popcorn   thirsty

unhappy   library

twenty   emergency

memory   fifty

seaweed

Lesson 113
Activity 6

ponies	thirsty	twenty
emergency	stories	cherries

1. Popcorn can make you **thirsty**.

2. Call Dad in an **emergency**.

3. Jenny likes to eat sweet **cherries**.

4. Thirty is more than **twenty**.

5. The **ponies** were nice to ride.

6. There are many **stories** to read in the library.

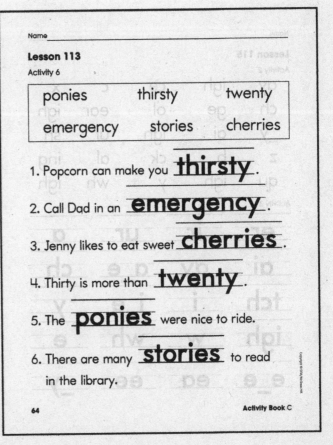

pony = **ponies**

penny = **pennies**

es lily = **lilies**

try = **tries**

fly = **flies**

fancy = **fancier**

thirsty = **thirstier**

er happy = **happier**

funny = **funnier**

Activity Book C   65

Bl<u>y</u>	better	<u>y</u>
dr<u>y</u>	ostr<u>ich</u>	sm<u>all</u>
anim<u>al</u>s	eagle	sky
myself	l<u>ie</u>	repl<u>ie</u>s
st<u>ick</u>	trees	lion
	<u>ch</u>imp	

66   **Activity Book** C

ay	igh	ce	c	x
ch	ge	ol	ear	igh
_y	ai	igh	ur	sh
z	b	ck	al	ing
qu	igh	y	wh	igh

Activity 3

er	**ir**	**ur**	**a**
ai	**ay**	**a_e**	**ch**
tch	**i**	**i_e**	**y**
igh	**w**	**wh**	**e**
e_e	**ea**	**ee**	**_y**

Activity Book C   67

pl<u>a</u>t<u>e</u>	m<u>ea</u>n
<u>wh</u>ite	s<u>qu</u>eeze
<u>s</u>eaweed	<u>v</u>isit
<u>pa</u>y	snail
tr<u>y</u>	fin<u>g</u>er
f<u>ar</u>mer	alwa<u>y</u>s
ever<u>y</u>	strin<u>g</u>

68   **Activity Book** C

Name

Lesson 115

_____ _____

_ng

_____

Activity 6

wing <u>**wing**</u> thing <u>**thing**</u>

ring <u>**ring**</u> spring <u>**spring**</u>

The king rang a gong.

<u>**The king rang a gong.**</u>

We sang a long song.

<u>**We sang a long song.**</u>

Activity Book C   **69**

Name

Lesson 116

Activity 1

igh	ing	ay	ee	er
ai	x	z	ol	qu
igh	u_e	tch	_dge	th
ong	ear	ce	ur	ck
ang	_y	b	are	_ng

Activity 3

thunde<u>r</u>	bright	cry	nee<u>d</u>s
<u>f</u>armer	<u>d</u>ark	cha<u>s</u>e	ban<u>k</u>
<u>H</u>ank	q<u>u</u>een	<u>s</u>heep	box<u>e</u>s
holding	tr<u>ai</u>n	cl<u>er</u>k

70   **Activity Book** C

Name

Lesson 116

Activity 4

<u>chunking</u>	<u>robber</u>	<u>farmer</u>
<u>hotbox</u>	<u>jumping</u>	<u>honking</u>
<u>racket</u>	<u>blanket</u>	<u>cranky</u>
<u>judge</u>	<u>something</u>	<u>police</u>
	<u>teacher</u>	

Activity Book C   **71**

Name

Lesson 116

Activity 5

1. Can you hear the girls <u>**sing**</u> ?
   sing sink

2. When I am sick, it is hard to <u>**think**</u> .
   thing think

3. <u>**Bring**</u> the blanket to the baby.
   Bring Brink

4. The bird's right <u>**wing**</u> is hurt.
   wing wink

5. I lost the <u>**ring**</u> from my finger.
   ring rink

6. The monkey can <u>**cling**</u> to the vine.
   cling clink

72   **Activity Book** C

Answer Key Activity Book C

53

Lesson 116
Activity 6

sell | time | Hank
honk | honked | hissed
hissing | chased | kept
police | lamp | very
over | bank | thanked

Lesson 117
Activity 2

er | ir | ur | tch
ch | j | ge | gi
dge | c | ck | k
s | ce | ci | a_e
ai | ay | i_e | y
igh | e_e | ea | ee
_y

Lesson 117
Activity 3

crazy | dragon | sky | car
wheel | cute | nice | paint
muddy | grand | letter | kitten
uncle | rice | eating

Activity 4

sing | song
sang | bring
try | tries
contest | began
open | wheel

Lesson 117
Activity 5

paint | painted | painting
bake | baked | baking
slip | slipped | slipping
rule | ruled | ruling

Activity 6

highway | whacker | grandson
checking | sending | thinking
thanking | thankful | thankfully
deliver | eating

Name _____

Lesson 118

Activity 1

ing	er	qu	igh	ai
f	i	i_e	ir	a
a_e	e	e_e	u	u_e
ch	le	_dge	v	ce
ck	x	igh	_y	ear
ong	ang	_ay	eer	ol

Activity 2

1. We (like) fresh cherries.

2. Six logs were on the (fire.)

3. That little (fly) tickles me.

4. Nick has a pink (necktie.)

5. The baby will (cry) if she is sleepy.

6. A (flashlight) will help you see in the dark.

Activity Book C   77

Name _____

Lesson 118

Activity 4

reading	qu<u>ack</u>	sn<u>ai</u>l	<u>h</u>olds
bo<u>x</u>	carry	carri<u>es</u>	<u>th</u>is
<u>s</u>ent	s<u>pee</u>d	speed<u>y</u>	might
<u>str</u>ong	<u>br</u>ing	r<u>ai</u>ned	

Activity 5

<u>hotbox</u>	<u>someone</u>	<u>whacker</u>
<u>sending</u>	<u>grandson</u>	<u>tickets</u>
<u>checking</u>	<u>fixing</u>	<u>fixes</u>
<u>deliver</u>	<u>delivering</u>	<u>platform</u>
<u>passage</u>		

78   **Activity Book** C

Name _____

Lesson 119

Activity 1

<u>**sing**</u>	<u>**train**</u>	<u>**sweet**</u>
<u>**child**</u>	<u>**fix**</u>	<u>**visit**</u>
<u>**toss**</u>	<u>**sent**</u>	<u>**sister**</u>
<u>**car**</u>	<u>**paper**</u>	<u>**quack**</u>

Activity 2

ju<u>dge</u>	c<u>o</u>ntest	b<u>e</u>gan	pi<u>e</u>
m<u>e</u>	<u>g</u>iant	r<u>u</u>les	che<u>ck</u>s
<u>br</u>ight	spray	sp<u>r</u>ang	d<u>r</u>y
gig<u>gl</u>e	mess<u>y</u>	<u>r</u>ight	

Activity Book C   79

Name _____

Lesson 119

Activity 3

1. Ellen **rode** in her car.
   rod   rode

2. The little **baby** began to cry.
   bab   baby

3. I hear the duck **quack** in the pond.
   quack   qack

4. She will **judge** the contest.
   jug   judge

5. A snail is not **speedy**.
   speedy   spedy

6. This is a **cute** cat.
   cute   cut

80   **Activity Book** C

Answer Key Activity Book C

55

Lesson 119
Activity 4

<u>vanilla</u>   <u>pudding</u>

family   <u>grocery</u>

<u>basketball</u>   Saturday

<u>yesterday</u>   <u>concert</u>

<u>flying</u>

Activity Book C   81

Lesson 120
Activity 1

king	late	wife
her	queen	tonight
might	bright	tie
dinner	told	squire
mayor	before	slice
	duchess	

82   **Activity Book** C

Lesson 120
Activity 2

some oh have was are half

onto here what to heard you

there said Mr. those says of

away does one again tonight

would two could Mrs. out four

want eight should bear these

water do hurray I'm today

they were too once your

oh no pull where put wrote

Activity Book C   83

Lesson 120
Activity 3

<u>princess</u>	<u>invite</u>	<u>never</u>
<u>duchess</u>	tonight	<u>reply</u>
<u>dinner</u>	<u>replied</u>	<u>before</u>

84   **Activity Book** C

Answer Key Activity Book C